ANDREW HILL
21 PIANO COMPOSITIONS

HENDON MUSIC

BOOSEY & HAWKES

AN IMAGEM COMPANY

DISTRIBUTED BY

HAL•LEONARD®
CORPORATION
7777 W. BLUEMOUND RD. P.O. BOX 13819 MILWAUKEE, WI 53213

www.boosey.com
www.halleonard.com

Published by Boosey & Hawkes, Inc.
229 West 28th Street
New York NY 10001

www.boosey.com

 an IMAGEM company

ISMN 979-0-051-24644-1
Printed in U.S.A. and distributed by Hal Leonard Corporation, Milwaukee WI
Notesetting by Randa Kirshbaum
First printed 2010

Quotes from Andrew Hill...

- On Sage-like Advice: "When you are by yourself you are almost forced to come up with a different approach."

interview with Greg Osby, "Reality Lessons," *DownBeat*, January, 2003

- On Composing: "I'm writing all of the time. And even when you have an arrangement, the performers' personalities take over the compositions... compositions don't have to be fixed... After you write them, then you get to know what the players will do, and you reshape... I get tired of hearing the same thing over and over again, and I enjoy my ability to change. Everything must change, or it just becomes part of the institutional retrospective."

interview with Bob Blumenthal, "Andrew Hill Seeks Synergy With His Sextet," *The Boston Globe*, April 30, 1999

- On Musical meaning: "The bird don't sing because it has a message, it sings because it has a song. I am responsible for telling a story in my music but not that responsible."

Jazz Times, January/February 2003

On Andrew Hill...

Andrew Hill's musical identity as a pianist and as a composer began to form when he first moved from Chicago to New York in 1962. Like Thelonious Monk, his playing and composing were inseparably integrated.

Although his music had melody, harmony and rhythm, his conception of each was so unique that he was categorized with the avant garde free form movement of that period. His music was avant garde in the strictest sense of the term, but it was anything but free form. As Monk was lumped into the bebop movement because he was there, so was Andrew put into the freedom bag. His music was free of cliché, but that was about the extent of it.

From the early sixties until his death in 2007, Hill amassed an amazing and prolific body of work with scores ranging from trio to jazz quartet with string quartet to large orchestra. His voice will live forever in his recordings and his compositions.

—Michael Cuscuna

It is with great humility that I lend my contribution to this collection of works by Andrew Hill, whom I consider to be one of the most profound and genuine artistic voices that this planet has ever produced. I am both honored and privileged to have been one of many who have been graced by his unshakable presence, detailed attention and advice; and my respect as well as admiration for him as an individual, mentor and friend only increases as his lessons ring more true today than ever before. Over the years I have logged countless numbers of hours listening to Andrew's music, marveling at his uncanny ability to weave tumultuous, peculiar and esoteric fragments and themes into artfully and masterfully hewn statements, each baring facets of his humanity that he neither avoided nor coveted.

In contemporary composition and improvised music circles, one of the most common but often inappropriately used terms is the word 'genius'. This designation, which is thrown about recklessly, has lost much of its legitimacy. Obviously, such a term cannot apply to every person that it is attached to, nor have many made breakthroughs in the multi-faceted discipline of this thing called music. True genius is indeed a rare phenomenon, and its characteristics are totally self-defining. However, I would contend that Andrew Hill is a most worthy candidate for such a declaration, given the profundity of his vast amounts of distinctive, creative works and the insightful gems of humanity that each one epitomizes.

It is not very common for a musician to mature into a unique and prolific force in their lifetime without an abundance of approval and support. It is even more rare that such a voice is forged within the overwhelming complacency and accommodation that exists in contemporary sonic art. The restless spirit that is Andrew Hill clearly exemplifies the unwavering pursuit of elusive and mysterious elements that he employed as frameworks for his well-devised sonic explorations. His continuing journey is one of wonder, a timeless story of joy and triumph set to music.

There have been many suggestions that Andrew's approaches to performance and composition were similar to other iconic predecessors. While this may be true to some extent, as it applies to most every developing and established artist who is in tune with the many contributors and innovators in modern expression, it is readily apparent that his thinking was much more probing, and full of reason and individuality to assert that he'd solely modeled himself on those that he'd admired. Any of his recorded performances clearly detail the musical triumphs of an advanced conceptualist who has mastered the fine art of musical storytelling, with one of the most passionate and original methods that has ever been developed.

Much has also been said and documented about the idiosyncratic nature of Andrew Hill's music, but to have a deep understanding, one must recognize how truly difficult it is to forge an original voice within the vast sea of emulation and complacency in modern music. Andrew would not adhere to that convention, nor allow the expectations of others to chart his creative course. Andrew's contributions to the contemporary improvised music canon are a series of separate, stylized conceptual breakthroughs. His usage of intricate, unconventional and hauntingly personalized harmonic, fragmented measures, whether in short form, combo writing, large ensemble or extended composition settings, vividly represents an uncompromising effort to challenge the accepted formulas of his era. Always identifiable, his technique and approach never fail to provide his associates with a bountiful array of options as he is a master of timing, placement, staging, sly decision-making and surprise. He is one of the foremost composers and stylists of our time, and the relevancy of his work cannot be overestimated.

In many ways Andrew was a mystic; a sage of sorts, given that he never answered my musical queries directly, but rather offered a multiplicity of choices or alternative referential information that I was obliged to process and decipher in my own time, for my own purposes. He relied on his charges and musicians to accept or reject his findings based upon their own requirements. Although initially frustrating, it was this methodology that I found to be ultimately the most gratifying and beneficial to my development as an artist. It was his unwavering pianistic touch and attention to nuance that propelled songs, which may have appeared as quirky and simplistic short stories, into lengthy, erratic and tumultuous excursions full of twisted logic and unpredictable musical consequences. These journeys were as exhilarating as they were unpredictable and challenging to any musician's risk-taking sensibilities. However, with all of the unexpected detours, each of Andrew's compositions bears elements of pure beauty and wonder, and reflects his distinctive curiosity and imagination. Stimulating, provocative, and wildly eclectic, each of his pieces represents exploration through his exceptional organization of sound.

I am grateful to have known him, and will continue to be inspired by his knowledge, wit and kindness.

—Greg Osby

To learn more about Andrew Hill, his compositions, and a full discography, please visit: http://andrewhilljazz.com/

This is a facsimile page of the original composition "Dusk" by Andrew Hill.

TABLE OF CONTENTS

15/8

Composed by Andrew Hill
transcribed by Ron Horton

ISMN 979-0-051-24644-1

15/8

To Solos (over Vamp)

After Solos, D.S. 𝄋 al *fine*

"15/8" was recorded on *Dusk* (Palmetto-2002). The personnel were
Marty Ehrlich and Greg Tardy, saxophones; Scott Colley, bass; Billy
Drummond, drums; and myself on Flugelhorn. – *RH*

ASHES

Composed by Andrew Hill
transcribed by Frank Kimbrough

"Ashes" appears on Greg Osby's album, *The Invisible Hand* (Blue Note),
and is one of only a few tunes we have in Andrew's distinctive hand. It's
a 19 bar form (4+5+6+4 bars) in medium tempo. – *FK*

On the Instrument:

"The piano has so many different things, you're always
a student of it. One year you try to perfect your percussion.
Now I am trying to perfect my dexterity. I'm still into
rhythm. It's a natural response. I'm instinctively working
on that stuff now."

interview with Greg Osby, "Reality Lessons," *DownBeat*, January, 2003

On Perfection:

"I just learned early on to strive for success, not perfection—
cause perfection a lotta times leaves you where you can't
enjoy anything."

Jet, May 13, 1985.

On Music:

"It doesn't hurt to have a guideline no matter what music you
are working in... The way I like to play is to perform each time
with a new piece of music or with some kind of different instru-
mentation... What I really want to do is play music."

interview with Don Heckman. "Roots, Culture and Economics,"
DownBeat, May 1966

BALL SQUARE

Composed by Andrew Hill
transcribed by Frank Kimbrough

Form: A A B

Solo on form

"Ball Square" has been recorded twice, the first in a trio setting on *Shades* (Soul Note), in a brisk swinging tempo that makes the triplets in bars 5 and 6 almost impossible to play with one hand. On its subsequent recording by the sextet on *Dusk* (Palmetto), it's played as a march at a much slower tempo. The B section always has a 12/8 blues feel for 6 bars before snapping back to the original tempo for 2 bars, and the 8 bar drum solo that ends the AAB (16+16+16 bar) form. During solos, the harmony on the A sections is sometimes treated as the first 8 bars of a 12 bar blues. The 8 bar drum solos at the end of each section are built into the form, and are included in solos. – FK

BOBBY'S TUNE

Composed by Andrew Hill
transcribed by Ron Horton

Bobby's Tune

"Bobby's Tune" was recorded on January 30, 1989 for Blue Note album, *Eternal Spirit*. The personnel were Greg Osby, saxophone; Bobby Hutcherson, vibes; Rufus Reid, bass; and Ben Riley, drums. – *RH*

CLAYTON GONE

Composed by Andrew Hill
transcribed by Frank Kimbrough

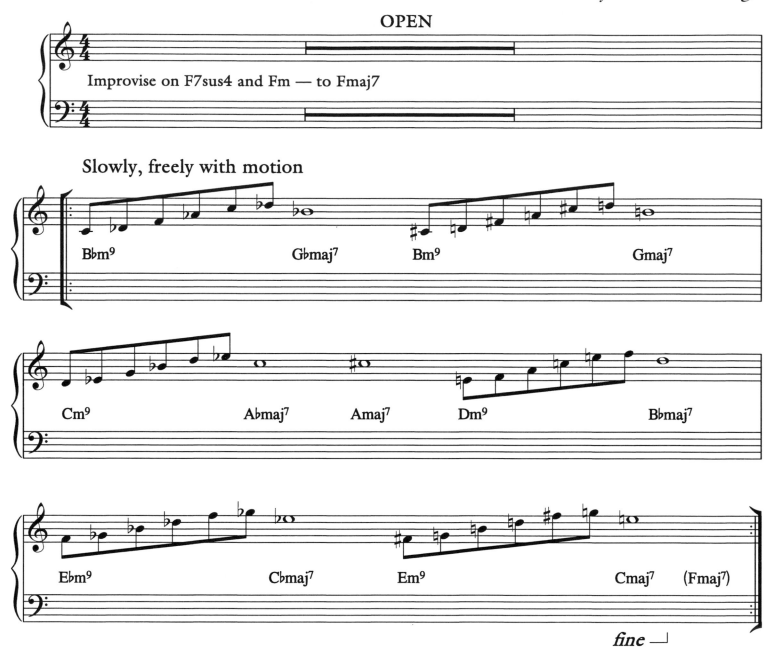

"Clayton Gone" was recorded in 1975, and appears on *Hommage* (East Wind), a solo recording released in Japan in 1975 and reissued on CD in 2000. It was finally released in the U.S. by Test Of Time Records in 2005. After the briefest hint of the melody, just a couple of cadences, the piece continues with a rhythmic improvisation, based on an F suspended dominant vamp, moving to F minor, and then finally to F major, lessening in rhythmic intensity before moving into the main body of the tune, which has an open form consisting of three (deceptive) cadences, then a chord to move it up a half-step, then three more cadences. It's a ruminative piece, played out of time, peacefully, but with forward motion. – *FK*

On Rhythm:

"Parker was important, and it was with him that I first
discovered that it is not enough to play melody, but
that rhythm is also important and that melody is rhythm."

interview with Seren Friis, translation, Paul Banks, *Jazz Special.*
April, 2003

On Titles:

"...If you're called a jazz artist you're locked into a
certain pigeon hole... It's all music. I can't see myself
locked into one harmonic or rhythmic conception."

interview with Chuck Berg, "Andrew Hill, Innovative Enigma,"
DownBeat. March, 1977

DOMANI

Composed by Andrew Hill
transcribed by Frank Kimbrough

Domani

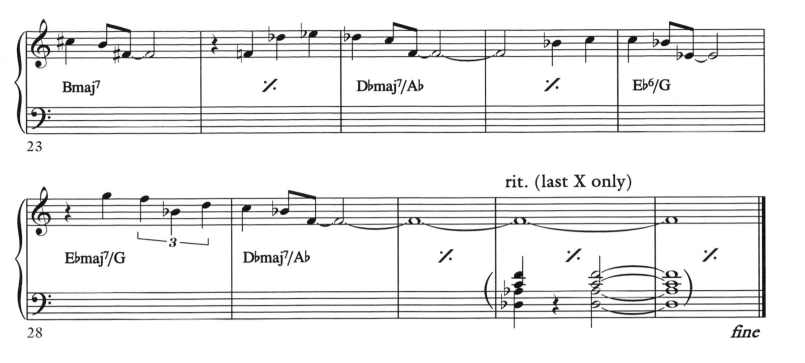

"Domani" ("tomorrow" in Italian) was recorded in Italy in 1986 for a trio and quartet album (*Shades*, on Soul Note). It's played extremely up tempo – somewhere around 300 beats a minute. It's a two section, 32 bar form, but is divided 14+18 instead of 16+16. The first section is two bars less than expected, which propels it into the second section, which has two extra bars more than expected, giving a slight breather before the succeeding chorus. – *FK*

DUSK

Composed by Andrew Hill
transcribed by Ron Horton

"Dusk" was first recorded on February 10 and 11, 1998 as a solo piano piece, and was released on *Les Trinitaires* (Jazz Friends Productions). On that CD, recorded over two nights, there are two versions of it. Later that year, when I was a member of Andrew's "Point of Departure Sextet," I wrote an arrangement where I included phrases from both of those solo piano versions. That sextet version appears on *Dusk* (Palmetto-2000). The personnel were Marty Ehrlich and Greg Tardy, saxophones; Scott Colley, bass; Billy Drummond, drums; and myself on flugelhorn. – *RH*

ERATO

Composed by Andrew Hill
transcribed by Ron Horton

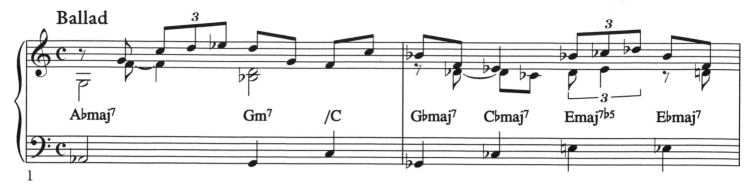

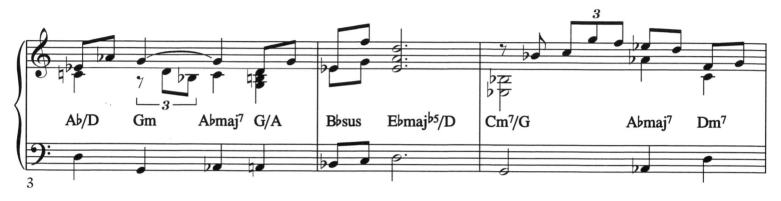

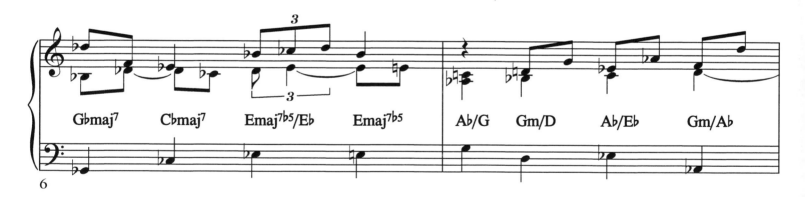

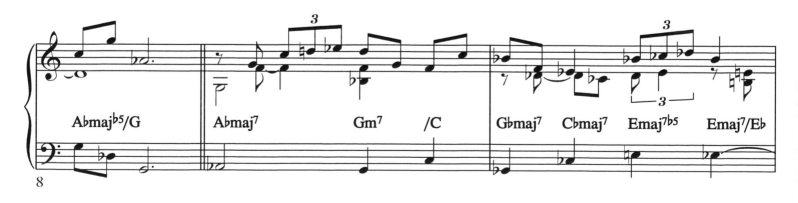

Erato

"Erato" was recorded as a trio on February 10, 1965 for Blue Note
album *One For One*. The session was not released until 1975.
"Erato's" original title was "Moon Chile." Richard Davis played
bass and Joe Chambers played drums. – *RH*

FROM CALIFORNIA WITH LOVE

Composed by Andrew Hill
transcribed by Frank Kimbrough

fine

"From California With Love" first appeared on the LP of the same name, recorded in 1978, and released on Artists House (AH9). Reissued on CD, Mosaic Select 23: *Andrew Hill – Solo*, it appears with two alternate takes with alternate titles: "Napa Valley Twilight" and "Above Big Sur." Andrew's original lead sheet is reproduced in the booklet accompanying the LP and CD set. It's in 3/4 time, with a one section, 20 bar form. On the recordings Andrew plays an E pedal under the changes indicated for the first 4 bars, though the lead sheet appears here as he wrote it. – *FK*

On Melody as Rhythm:

"If everything is rhythm, then you just have these rhythms on top of each other. But they're not polyrhythms or pyramids of rhythms, they're crossing rhythms."

interview with Ben Ratliff, "The Jazz Ear," *New York Times: Books,* 2008

On the Piano:

"I've made it a project to figure out how to record the piano. The key is not to approach it as an accompanying instrument. Instead of instruments accompanying each other, have equal volume on so they all stand on their own."

interview with David Adler, "Once More," *Jazz Times,* April, 2006

GOLDEN SUNSET

Composed by Andrew Hill
Transcribed by Jason Moran

Golden Sunset

fine

Golden Sunset

Golden Sunset

75

78

This tune appears on Andrew's album *Eternal Spirit* (Blue Note.)

Andrew's thoughts about rhythm were that rhythm was malleable. He thought of time/tempo as a bubble, and you could divide the bubble into any shape and size you wanted. The rhythms above are approximate.

Andrew's solo continues into a flurry of large clusters which are more gestural than specific. This solo really encapsulates Andrew's small intervallic movements that have come to define his sound. – *JM*

GONE

Composed by Andrew Hill
transcribed by Frank Kimbrough

"Gone" was first recorded in 1990, and appears as one of two solo performances on *But Not Farewell* (Blue Note). It also appears in a group performance on Reggie Workman's *Summit Conference* (Postcards), recorded in 1993. This transcription is from the Blue Note recording, on which it's played expansively, in a loose, stream-of-consciousness style. The improvisation is based on the second part of the tune, with an occasional allusion to the beginning few bars, returning to the written melody and playing it through once more to end the piece. – *FK*

HATTIE

Composed by Andrew Hill
transcribed by Frank Kimbrough

"Hattie" appears on *Nefertiti* (East Wind/Test of Time), and is named for Andrew's mother. It's one of his many waltzes, a simple, well-constructed 20 bar form, with plenty of room to play around with the written rhythms. It's a rollicking, playful, joyous tune. – *FK*

MIST FLOWER

Composed by Andrew Hill
transcribed by Frank Kimbrough

"Mist Flower" was recorded in 1975 and appears on *Blue Black*, first released on LP in Japan by East Wind, and later issued in the U.S. on CD by Test of Time Records. This tune has a one section, 15 bar form, with a straight-eighth note feel in medium tempo, with flute playing the melody. This tune should not be confused with an entirely different tune, also called "Mist Flower," which appears on Andrew's trio recording *Strange Serenade* (on Soul Note). – *FK*

NAKED SPIRIT
a.k.a. "Tripping"

Composed by Andrew Hill
transcribed by Frank Kimbrough

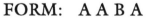

FORM: A A B A

"Tripping," from *Shades* (Soul Note), is played with a Latin "2" feel.
It's a **32** bar, AABA form, and the melody is played with loose rhythm.
It also appears in a solo version on *Hommage* (East Wind/Test Of
Time) with an alternate title ("Naked Spirit") played in a different
key (B♭ minor), with a slower feel, somewhat similar to a tango. – *FK*

NEFERTITI
a.k.a. "Nefertisis"

Composed by Andrew Hill
transcribed by Frank Kimbrough

FORM: A A B A
for Solos: A Section - E Natural minor; B section - D Dorian

"Nefertiti" is from the album of the same name, originally issued on LP in 1978 by East Wind (Japan), and released in the U.S. the following year by Inner City Records. It was reissued on CD by East Wind in 2002, and in the U.S. by Test Of Time Records in 2005. With a slightly different title ("Nefertisis"), and played in a different key (D minor), it appears on Andrew Hill's first solo album, *Live at Montreux*, recorded in July of 1975, and released on LP by Arista/Freedom. It was later reissued on CD by Freedom. It has an AABA, 32 bar form, and sounds like a processional— very regal and stately, slow and steady. – *FK*

NICODEMUS

Composed by Andrew Hill
transcribed by Frank Kimbrough

"Nicodemus" appears on *But Not Farewell* (Blue Note), and is essentially a blues form with altered chord changes, repeated to make a 24 bar form with first and second endings. It's in 5/4 meter, and the chord changes in the last 4 bars of each 12 bar section vary significantly from the changes one usually associates with the blues. Andrew's lead sheet is in G, and doesn't indicate first and second endings. The transcription presented here is in the key in which it was recorded (F), and indicates first and second endings, as well as a few notes that are played differently on the CD than indicated on Andrew's lead sheet, which may have been changed at the recording session. – *FK*

On "Nicodemus":

"One of my forays into 5/4."

Piano Jazz, NPR, 2005

On Cultural Support, 1966:

"If a place like Lincoln Center can be built for
classical music, why can't another place be built
for people who are a product of this society?"

interview with Nat Hentoff. "The New Jazz," *The New York
Times Magazine*, December 20, 1966

SAMBA RASTA

Composed by Andrew Hill
transcribed by Jason Moran

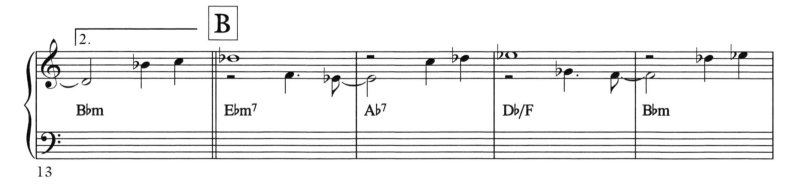

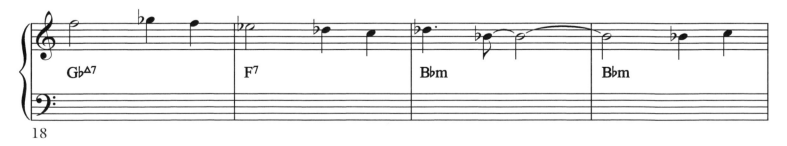

Samba Rasta

22

26 *fine*

Solos: A   A   B

This tune is from the album *Eternal Spirit* (Blue Note).

When I moved to New York in 1993, I saw the Andrew Hill Quartet
perform at the Village Vanguard. I'll never forget hearing "Samba Rasta."
Andrew melded reggae rhythms with jazz harmonies. Having the steady
reggae rhythm makes it clear how evolved Andrew's rhythmic concept was. *– JM*

TOUGH LOVE

Composed by Andrew Hill

transcribed by Frank Kimbrough

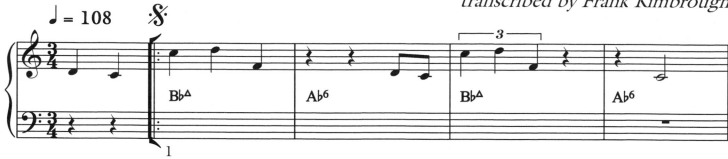

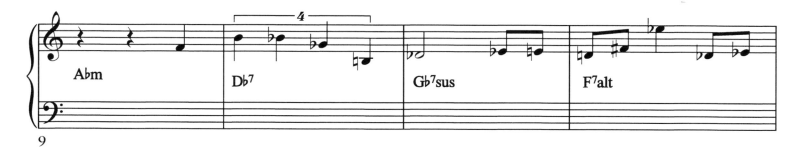

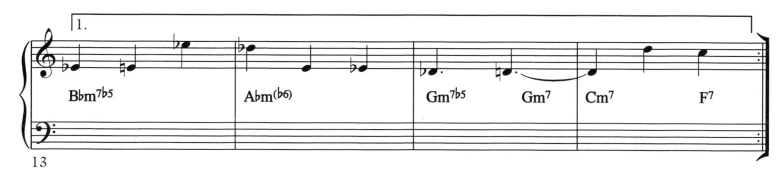

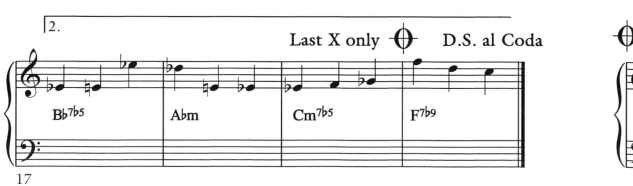

"Tough Love" is in two parts – when Ron Horton and I discussed this tune, we were confused until we realized that we had been thinking about two different tunes. (This is not unusual given Andrew's penchant for re-titling pieces, or for giving two pieces the same title.) Later on, I remembered a conversation in which Andrew had referred to the *Tough Love Suite*, so perhaps that explains our initial confusion. This transcription is from Greg Osby's *Invisible Hand* (Blue Note), recorded in 1999, and one of Andrew's few recorded sideman appearances. A solo piano version also appears on *Dusk* (Palmetto), also from 1999, where it's played in a much looser fashion. It's a 2 part, 16+16 bar form, but with irregular phrasing (each section is 5+5+6 bars). – *FK*

TOUGH LOVE (Part 2)

Composed by Andrew Hill
transcribed by Ron Horton

"ToughLove (Part 2)" is the other part to Andrew's Tough Love Suite.
This part was performed frequently by the sextet, but never recorded.
Andrew often made "suites" by combining several compositions together,
linked by improvisational material. This part was recorded by the big band
as a portion of the composition/suite "New Pinnochio," which appears on
A Beautiful Day (Palmetto-2002). – *RH*

VERONA RAG

Composed by Andrew Hill
transcribed by Jeffrey Lovell

Verona Rag

Transition

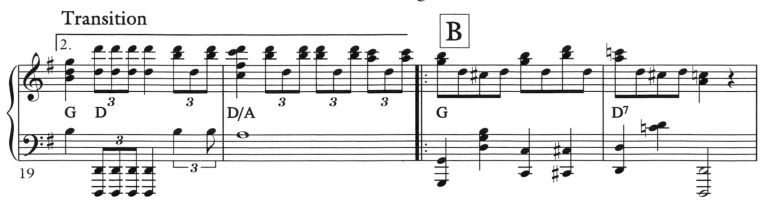

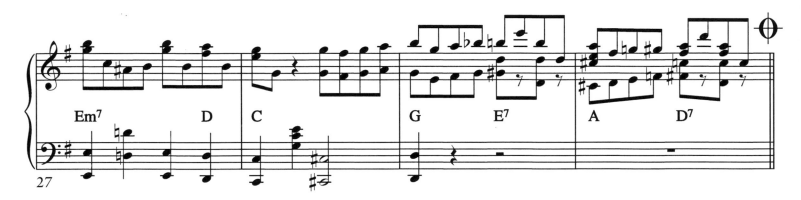

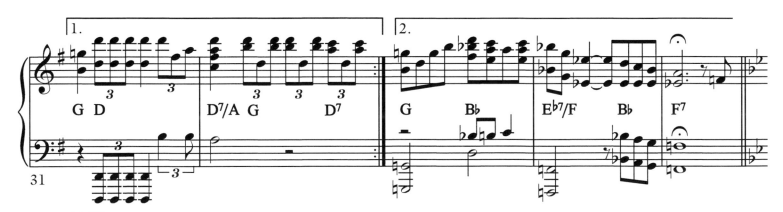

Verona Rag

Verona Rag

Verona Rag

The entire form repeats from here.

Sections C, D, E & F are altered on the repeat.
After the repeat, the A & B sections are repeated
once more before the Tag.

This transcription is an interpretation of the primary melodic and harmonic gestures of "Verona Rag." It does not attempt to account for the innumerable variations that Hill improvises over each of the six strains, but it rather identifies the compositional framework that Hill masterfully reworks as the piece progresses. Significantly, the first two strains are the least varied of all the strains as they contain embedded melodic material from the spiritual, "I've Decided to Make Jesus My Choice," which is the inspirational source for "Verona Rag." – *JL*

WESTBURY

Composed by Andrew Hill
transcribed by Frank Kimbrough

"Westbury" was recorded in 1990, and appears on *But Not Farewell* (Blue Note). It's a waltz, with an AAB (8+8+16 bars) form, scored for a front line of soprano saxophone and trombone. It has a breezy, elegant feel. – *FK*

Andrew Hill – Pianist and Composer

Legendary pianist and composer Andrew Hill defied categorization for over four decades with his enigmatic and sophisticated musical style. He was hailed by *The New York Times* as "one of the 1960's jazz heroes" and was alternately referred to as a genius and a master by critics and colleagues alike. Born in Chicago on June 30, 1931, he began teaching himself to play piano at 10 and was later introduced by Bill Russo to composer/theorist Paul Hindemith. Mr. Hill was honored with a Lifetime Achievement Award from the Jazz Foundation of America (1997), received the international JAZZPAR Award (2003), and was named Jazz Composer of the Year five times by the Jazz Journalists Association. A champion of Hill's music, the late Blue Note Records founder, Alfred Lion, proclaimed Hill his "last great protégé" and produced his early classics for the label, including *Point of Departure*. With over 40 recordings over just as many years, Hill consistently astounded listeners with his unorthodox compositions. His nonet album, *Passing Ships*, recorded in 1969 for mixed winds, brass, and a rhythm section, enjoyed much attention and acclaim when it was rediscovered and released for the first time in 2003 (the music also received its first public performance at Merkin Hall in 2006). His recording *Dusk* (Palmetto, 2000) received critical raves and several "album of the year" awards. Hill's final release, *Time Lines* (Blue Note, 2006), was voted Best Jazz Album by *DownBeat* magazine.

In the months following his passing on April 20, 2007, he was the posthumous recipient of several honors, including an honorary doctorate of music degree from the Berklee College of Music, induction into the DownBeat Hall of Fame, and three awards from the Jazz Journalists Association: Composer of the Year (2007), Pianist of the Year (2007), and the Lifetime Achievement Award in Jazz. Hill joined the ranks of such lauded composers as Stravinsky, Copland, Elliott Carter, as well as jazz luminaries David Benoit and Chick Corea by signing with renowned music publisher Boosey & Hawkes. He received the nation's highest honor in jazz, the NEA Jazz Masters Award in 2008.